Universal Manifestation Journal

By

Monica Earl Washington

BOBM PUBLISHING, LLC.

2022

UNIVERSAL MANIFESTATION JOURNAL

Powerful Ways to Manifest a New Reality in 30 Days

MONICA EARL WASHINGTON

First Printing: 2021

ISBN: 979-8-9860894-8-5

Ordering Information:

Special discounts are available on quantity purchases
by corporations, associations, educators, and others.
For details, contact the publisher at the above-listed
address.

U.S. trade bookstores and wholesalers: Please contact
info@businessofbooksmastermind.com

DEDICATION

This book is dedicated to my sons; my oldest Mr. James "Tank" Earl and my youngest Mr. Reginald Kilo Banks as I began to write this Journal for my sons. God blessed my womb to birth only twice within my life and I am truly grateful and honored to be called "Ma, Mom, Mama and Mother." My walk within life has everything to do with birthing and raising my sons, for any and all of the challenges I had as mother to raise and provide for my sons, giving all I had to my sons who has never seen a struggle as long as God prepared the way for me to 100% provide and raise my sons, I dedicate this journal to the Kings of Kings within my life, and to my oldest son children, my grandchildren, *Mr. Corinthian Earl* and *Ms. Naomi Earl*, my Queen.

I cannot tell you enough, how much I love my children, as my prayer daily is that God richly bless you with the greatest and finest things that money can never purchase and that you know the value of what is really important: LOVE.

To my sons and my grandchildren, I love you with every breath that I breathe in me. I am with honor to have such a high calling of "Mother" upon my life and to be called "Ma, Mom, Mama and Mother," of the precious gifts bestowed upon me.

Last but not least I send my dedication and love to my late grandparents Mr. Robert Eugene Johnson Sr and Mrs. Rosester Hoosier Johnson, the heart and soul of my life, my book and my products. The true King and Queen, real role models who truly loved me genuinely.

CONTENTS

ACKNOWLEDGMENTS

Thanks to all of the people who prayed for Monica during the time of the world's deadly virus pandemic of COVID-19. Special love to my father, my daddy, God, Lord Jesus Christ, the Commander in chief of my life, with the almighty guidance of the Holy Spirit as a teacher and faithful guide to push and birth out this journal. This Journal was not only written during the world deadliest virus; this journal was birth through pain of betrayal, hate and intentional plans and plots to destroy and bury Monica; which led to Monica rebuilding stronger under the walk of faith, shoes of peace, replacing the helmet of salvation, with a sharpen sword I united stronger with of the King James Bible, to hurdle over hot coals and stones deliberately placed and staged by enemies as strong as Pharaoh's army against Monica to die in the midst of the Red Sea during the crisis of the COVID-19. Special thanks to Mr. Sugar Ray Destin, owner of Business of Books Mastermind (BOBM), for hearing my cry, while viewing my cry to publish my very own first published book through this outstanding and amazing publishing company, to include his new wife Mrs. Chimere Bacon Destin, owner of BossUp Houston, for the beautiful creation and management of Monica Earl Washington website for Neecy's Soft and Sweet Holistic Organic Southern Scents.

I also would like to acknowledge my dearest Sisters, I am in tears as I write these following names my dearest and long times family *Ms. Crista "Shotzie" Shanklin Clairborne, Ms. Debbie Williams Lanier, Ms. Amanda Huntley Dunsenberry, Ms. Charlsie Hand, Ms. Monica Guthridge Trigueros, Ms. Angela Fisher (my Pentagon got it together sister), Ms. Dee Talton,* my dearest brothers, *Mr. Michael "Rebop" Stevenson, Mr. Jermaine Speigh*t (Walter Reed Army Medical Center will always be in our hearts),

Fort Belvoir Community Hospital EMCOR Harley Davidson riding silently employees (brothers in Christ) and my dearest and best neighbors ever of *Mr. and Mrs. Jane Hundall.* You all play one of the biggest major role during the cruelest infiltration of a staged and planned attack upon a human's life during the deadliest time of the world and you all know the very greatest and largest things you all individually did for me from the purest of the heart, seeking nothing in return, during my time of the hardest trial and tribulations of plotted hindrances within my life. Thank you all.

My last acknowledgement goes out to *Alexandria, VA, Junior Female Ushers (JFU),* my pray and walk your way out, faithfulness of God cancels worry and from mess to a miracle sisters, thank you for the most powerful and meaningful thing to me while in the walk to cross the Red Sea, daily, openly and private prayers. *Psalm 145:14; "The Lord upholdeth all that fall, and raiseth up all those that be bowed down.* I am up with God now JFU!

WHAT YOU NEED TO KNOW TO START

> How to start this fasting and manifestation manual for success
> Fast/meditation time should be 2, 4, 6, 8, 10, 12 hours. Make time for you to be alone. You will need the time to become at peace, write it all down from beginning to end. The good, bad, ugly and cute. This is the start of a new you moving forward to a better you.
> The main goal by the end of week 4, you should be able to do one full day of a 12 hour fast, for experts in fasting with no health issues of pregnant should be able to do a 12 hour fast for up to 3 to 5 days during the 4th week.
> Whatever you do, please don't lie to yourself, don't place yourself in an ignoring position of your truths to clean up and move to a better you.
> Best time to start is early am morning hours. This is where you must *sacrifice*. The main goal is to search and clean up yourself to manifest in the greatness you truly desire. You must sacrifice to be awake in the consistent times that you chose to fast, purge, connect spiritually, that will lead to great manifestation.
> Early am hour's to start *(12am, 4am, 5am, 6am)* and (8pm, 9pm, 10pm, 11pm). These are the best time of day as the day is not noisy and/or busy. Calming down times.
> If you choose another time of the day, it must be a consistent and committed time with no interruptions that will cause or lead you into distractions and disruption from fasting and meditation. Turn off phones, televisions, laptop/computer alerts and all distractions. It is best to be consistent. It is best to be in a silent and quiet place.

WHAT IS SPIRITUAL FASTING? LET'S LEARN ABOUT FASTING

- To abstain from food, liquids, television, cell phones, profanity, negative conversation, sex, no social media, anything that will break your concentration to reach the renewing of the purpose of cleaning/cleansing up yourself to manifest what you truly desire
- Fasting is a private individual journey as one must be discipline to see the public reward of action results of remaining consistent
- Discipline consistent fasting removes barriers, allowing your spirit within you to communicate with God without any disturbance, while establishing a direction connection for your soul to connect to righteousness of the Higher God
- Fasting helps to loosen heavy bondage, tear down stronghold of the daily life journey that can fall upon one's life
- Fasting is one the most powerful ways to connect with the higher God for healing and restoration to the supernatural power of the higher God for fulfillment of restoration of healing of the mind, body and soul.
- Fasting can influence positive character, speech, thinking, behavior of your daily life journey, clearing the way for one to have victory
- Fasting is very beneficial in discipline your mind and flesh from addictions, drugs, alcohol, lust, sex, cigarettes, gambling, profanity, an much more wrongful intents that are not of good morals, values and sound judgement
- Fasting empowers deliverance from strong holds, bondages, while instilling strength, faith and wisdom into stronger

integrity, compassion, righteous morals, values and making righteous sound decisions

- Fasting empowers one to tune into quietness to hear the gentle voice of God, allowing your flesh to submit to the authority of the gentleness of God, opening up your spirit to receive the supernatural power of God
- Fasting reinforces effective daily prayer life that must be preserved from pride to fully cleanse to manifest
- For beginners in fasting it is not suggest that one start out daily on 2 to 3 hours during the 1st week, 3-4 hour during the 2nd week, 4-6 hours during the 3rd week and 6-8 hours during the 4th week. During the last week you must sacrifice to meet the goal before going into manifestation, you must purge out all negative energy before you can manifest any positive righteous energy to manifest.
- If you have health issues and pregnant, you must start as a *"New Born." The "New Born"* can only go a limited amount of hours due to licensed professional medication prescribed that requires food to be eaten at a certain time with the instructions of the medication, as well as women that are pregnant and nursing mothers
- The *"New Born"* would start out of the hours of 2-4 hours for the entire 4 weeks of this fasting manifestation journal and under the medical guidance advice of a Physician.
- The "New Born, must follow food guidelines for established consistent fasting days according to medical and medication instructions
- Here a couple of effective fasting that I have completed:
- *Normal/Simple fast*-No food or liquid during the duration of the fast.
- Example: Monday, fast start time 12am-2am, (while awake), no food, liquid, televisions, cell phones, profanity, sex, negative conversation, iPad, laptops, apple watches, anything that would

cause any distractions to break your conversation; this is where the sacrifice begins. FYI-There will be many attempts of distractions that will come out of nowhere to break your discipline and concentration when you begin your fast. One must remain discipline to fast before going into manifesting greatness. You don't want to take *sewer water* to make a pitcher of *grape Kool-Aid.* It will be contaminated and contaminations will lead to other things that will make one severely sick. This is what will happen if you don't fast to purge out all of the negative nasty energy away from your mind, body and soul. You can manifest great things into your life that will only be limited editions into an infested swamp of hungry alligators that will gulp your great manifestation within hours or before you will be able to truly enjoy the greatness of manifestation.

- Absolute/Supernatural fast-No food or liquids during the duration of the fast. This is a *40 day fast* or more fasting. *Deuteronomy 9:9,(NKJB)* when Moses went into the mountain, Moses was away for 40 days and 40 nights in the presence of God, who wrote the first set of the "Ten Commandments," that was written with the finger of God, for the people to be in obedience, Moses did not eat or drank for the duration of the time away. This fast requires strong discipline, concentration with a purpose. Moses came back with the first set of the "Ten Commandments. Your individual purpose could be seeking clarity or strategy for your life, there could be an immediate crisis of trouble that has knocked on your door to cause a stronghold in your life, your children, or you may be seeking a deeper rooted religious walk within your life.

- *Hinduism*-One of the most powerful things I love about this religion is the "Yoga." I know of two that I love and have tried, which is the *"Raja and the Bhakti Yoga."* The main purpose of the "Yoga" is be in profound quietness with no interruptions and focus on one's mental control, purity that clams the mind. Hinduism yoga practices, one must be very discipline while practicing yoga to see a divine positive paths to God, which the Hinduism religion believe God presence is around and felt all around the world and in people. For the Christianity, it is the fasting, calming the mind, body and soul being in a quiet place to connect with positive energy to receive the positive supernatural voice from the higher God to move into a positive direction.

- *Daniel fast*-No food or liquids for the duration of the fast. The Daniel fast I began up to 21 days my first time, but it can go 30 or 40 days as one desire their spiritual religious purpose. This is a fast that one can start in the suggested early am or pm hours while some people have a specific meal of the day that one omitted (breakfast, lunch, dinner) or any other food that you desire to omit. There are some people that omit breakfast and lunch or other strong emphasis on the restriction of food and liquids intake. *In Daniel 10:2-3 (NKJB),* Daniel was fasting from choice foods as he was seeking clarity and understanding from God, as Daniel was practicing self-discipline seeking understanding from God. Islam-One of the most powerful thing I love about the Islamic faith is the how they connect to the biblical book teaching from the Quran, where this faith calls out to the higher God "Allah." This faith teaches that praying five times a day is for one to be together in love and be thankful for life, for purification where it is taught in the Islamic faith that one must refrain from indecency and any wrong actions for spiritual nourishment and growth. The other powerful thing that I love about the Islamic faith is during the 9th month of the year, the Islamic faith go into a fasting Ramadan that starts at dawn to dust, refraining from all food and liquids during the day light hours, with added instructions for one that may have medical conditions and pregnant/nursing mothers; it is in the Islamic faith that the main purpose of seeking in the religious faith is to open one up to have an established relationship with God, learning self-discipline and self-control and having empathy for the less fortune during the fasting 9th month, while they move in with strong encouraging actions of generosity to the less fortune. There is always a purpose in fasting and meditation. What is your Why? What do you want or desire?

- Fasting suggested musical selections-It is vital that when fasting with music if one desires to have light music playing. I always suggest that light music with no word. Why no words? Words can cloud thoughts, create distractions with the wrong words. Instrumental soft Christian musical selections that I have found comfortable, relaxing, helps me to stay focus on my fast with the ability to write in my personal journal that is easily found on YouTube such as:

- Acoustic Christian instrumental guitar hymns.

- Heavenly Christian instrumental harp.

- Sounds of waves-ocean with seagulls

- Calm piano 24/7

- Most of these musical selections are soft, gentle to the mind, body and soul. Soft, calming and breathtaking.

- Breaking of Fast-Intake of food is vital when on a fast. Major thing to remember when coming off the fast:

- Avoid food high in carbs and sugar. I have learned it will create anxiety and heartburns.

- Consume food slowly.

- Consume easily digestible food in small portions such as: rice, lean meat like turkey, skinless chicken, fish, applesauce, eggs, instant oatmeal, yogurt, and yogurt is very high in protein and great for the digestive system. These are many of things I always have available when I am fasting ready when I come off the fast. I normally prepare, rice, baked lemon chicken and broccoli. Small portions.

- It is not good to break a fast with a feast or buffet style menu. I have learned from experience that it will have you feeling very uncomfortable, feeling bloated, congested and it cause severe heart burns.
- It is not wise to drink alcohol, beer, liquor, and wine after coming off of a fast.
- Healthy snacks-I have always prepared light healthy snacks and have them ready when I come off of fasting such as: applesauce, fresh apples, you can cut up apples and put peanut butter on the apple slices, smoothies with kale in the smoothies, hummus and fresh veggies, and my favorite is avocado toast, and last black beans and corn salsa with light tortilla chips. Great snack that are easy to consume, easy to pack and go and light weight on the digestive system.
- Drink plenty of water
- There are many ways to break a fast in a healthy ways. The most important thing about breaking a fast is having food ready and available after the completion of the fast. Take the time to schedule your days of fasting and have food prepared and ready. This will stop you from being scattered, racing to go get food, when your body will light coming off a fast.

THE TRUTHS: DAYS 1-10

This is where you cleanse yourself and admit and write all of your wrong(s) that you have wronged with anyone or anything that you know that caused strife, hardship, persecution through gossip, laughter, finger pointing through persecution by being evil, under handed that led to one's hurt and pain through you or your doings.

This is where you dig and search your entire self. If you have any bitterness, jealousy, envy, hate, regrets that led to resentment, betrayal, pain, molestation/raped, private drug, alcohol, sexual addiction, loss of love one that you never grieved, deepened rooted backlogged pain that you never released, anything that takes your mind away in pain and anger that stagnates your "Being Great," this is the time of week one to search, address yourself truthfully and go into cleansing and fasting and write your truth down.

This is where you look deep within yourself, face your truths. Look in the mirror at you to fix your truth. Write it down, you have to be honest with yourself and push out all negative energy out before you can move on within your life or the next phase of this journal.

This is where you speak to God, or the higher God you serve. God is God of good, with directions of good that teaches one to do right unto others as you want it done unto you. Telling God that you want to release and turn away from old bad habits of life, wrongful negative people or anything that is weighing you down that you have done and only you have done and no one humanly knows what you have done that was so blood gushing wrong; you want to be free to fix it and follow God, or the higher God you serve that lead to you doing what is right and telling God, or the higher God that you serve that you want to become a new individual to become a positive motivate individual in God through baptism or other religious faith baptism or confession and receiving the Holy renewed Spirit.

Investing your life in a strong religious base ministry to help you maintain a lasting life in God. Accepting God as your savior, walking in faith on a new path and know that as you repent and ask for forgiveness, it is done through God as you walk on faith to rejoin into a faith based ministry for growth to seek out your soul salvation.

There are many religions that one practice, I practice Christianity. I read from the King James Bible, that teaches me to fast, meditate on God's goodness, treating people right, refrain from judgment of people, gossiping, mistreatment, accepting my wrongs and straightening my wrongs with the individual I may have wronged, and corrections through following spiritual and man laws, however, there are many that practice other religions that I have come to learn they all adore a "God,' that is divine in teaching individuals to do what is good and right, fast and meditate to seek the righteous path on one's life's journey. Self-educating of study I have reviewed, attended and learn in religion is that in the end, religion is a religion where people come together seeking self-improvement within their life on a religious Christianity life seeking the adoration of a higher God for the afterlife. All religion may instruct from different concepts, but it all comes out to all seeking to do what is good and right unto mankind. Let's look below.

WORLD RELIGION:

It is safe to say that this is a vast and touchy subject. Many are with strong faith in a high God, some are skeptic and there are some that are just in between spirituality. Nevertheless, every human being desire an area within their life to seek peace that will produce cultural constructs of power dynamics that can produce philosophical innovation, ethical reform as one move in the world. World religion is organized on a belief system that individuals uphold in a higher power. Having an understanding of world religion promotes an analytical and empathetic approach to religion with an informed understanding of the diversity of world religions. The greatest thing about self-educating oneself about world religion it will foster a respectful awareness of the beliefs and practices of the faith members of the various religions in the world and it is here one can develop an understanding of how religion affects people lives with a global appreciation of the many strong issues that surround the spiritual beliefs, controversies and the way people move in the world today that also promotes responsible and greatly informed international respect. As I set out to self-educate about world religion, I began this journey of learning in year my youngest son Reginald K. Banks was abruptly born in my life through inappropriate medical care in 1993 and abruptly separating from my oldest son James R. Earl, due to the many severe health issues my youngest son was unfairly born into, I realize that as I was meditating and fasting in my Christianity beliefs, that I was surrounded by many that had no religious faith and many that had religious faith that was unknown unto me and I was not sure what the many high tech medical team surrounded by my youngest son was performing in medical care unto my youngest son.

I have come to learn that classification of world religion can be problematic due to the arbitrary of constructions of the indigenous of religions that makes it very easy for ideological manipulation, if one chose not to truly learn that the world is surrounded by millions of people who are not studying the same religious faith as yourself, however, that does not make people bad people if people decide to establish religious beliefs that collaborates to do what is good and right through other teaching outside of the religious faith one believes.

Some may say that religion is impossible to encapsulate. However, for the many that are strong in their religious faith will say it is not impossible to encapsulate. Now let's look at the many various religions, all religions collaborate with personal individual meditation, seeking peace within which is what all religions teaches to individuals within their religious teachings:

Christianity-monotheistic religion: Studies from the King James Bible and believes the Father (God), the son (Jesus) and the Holy Ghost (Biblical Guidance).

Bahá'í Faith: is essentially a spiritual ideology that does teach all religions focusing on the espousing the importance of unity and universal equality and believes in Bahá'u'lláh as the founding religious figure with a main teaching of goals of a unified world order that ensures the prosperity of all nations to include races and creeds.

Buddhism: a religion whose traditional teaching beliefs on the ideas of moral rectitude with the freedom release from material attachments striving for peace through meditation with the main focus of self-control through meditation; while focusing on wisdom, kindness and compassion to mankind. Meditation is very well known practice in Buddhism.

Hinduism: a religion with teaching and beliefs that the human being is not confined to the body or the mind, but connected through the spark of God within one's soul connecting spiritually through peace, joy and wisdom united with and through God, with practices of meditation through "Yoga," to gain full positive meditation of individual establishment of one's self through inner spirit to connect to God who is called Brahman, with the divine essence of Atman, with teaching of the Vedas. Hinduism believes in the law of cause and effect that individuals creates on one journey by ones thoughts, words and deeds that is called "Karma." Hinduism teaching also includes personal discipline, good conduct, purification, and meditation as life is sacred to be loved and revered through pure love, light, deserving tolerance and understanding to all mankind.

Islam: a monotheistic religion that believes "Allah" is the only God and Muhammed is the messenger; who study from the "Quran," that teaches that good behavior and adherence will lead to a promising afterlife in paradise, and one disregards one will be led to damnation. It is important that one pray 5 times a day at a particular time in peace and quiet and make a trip to the holiest site to gain spiritual strength, to include the practice of the 5 pillar of Islam faith.

Judaism: a religion that teaches from the "Torah," that teaches that God spoke to Abraham of the omnipotence of God, and considered the first prophet of Judaism. The most important teachings of Judaism is there is only one God and the teaching wants people to do what is just and right with being compassionate. One of the most powerful Judaism teaching is the Jewish Holy Days, a day is established as a physical rest for the body, mind and soul with main focus on spiritual renewal for one to restore strength and stronger relationship with God to build up the family and "labor" is prohibited on the Sabbath, to include prohibition of doing business, shopping, and housework. Jewish Sabbath day is nurtured in meditation of prayer, resting peacefully, while reflecting on joyful connections with God in meditation of peaceful prayer to rise and do what is right and treat all mankind with love

Fasting and Meditation Scriptures to start with your truths:
Acts 3:19 "Now repent of your sins and turn to God, so that your sins may be wiped away." (NKJB)

2 Chronicles 7:14 "Then if my people who are called by my name will humble themselves and pray and seek my face and turn from their wicked ways, I will hear from heaven and will forgive their sins and restore their land." (NKJB)

2 Corinthians 5:17 "Therefore if any man be in Christ, he is a new creature: old things are passed away; behold, all things are become new." (NKJB)

Judaism-Torah structured teachings "Deuteronomy 28:1-14, speaks of the blessings of obedience; "And if you faithfully obey the voice of the Lord your God, being careful to do all his commandments that I command you today, the Lord your God will set you high above all the nations of the earth. The Torah teaching instructs that people have responsibilities to God and humankind of being kind, be honest, if you are in leadership one should be a great leader and respectful to humankind in the work force, be compassionate while striving to be a good citizen. "Mindfulness," is very powerful in Judaism, it is a practice to "Meditate." Fasting in many other religious organization to establish connection and strengthen ones spiritual journey, that many of the Judaism feels it is a way of "improving the planet, while putting the attention on God, removing "self" out the way to build a strong relationship with God involving a personal encounter with God through prayer, fasting and studying the instructed teaching of the Torah. One must be truthful with themselves when dealing with their own personal truths with meditating and fasting into a righteous path for betterment of life is what is teachings are taught in the Torah religion.

Bahá'í Faith structured teachings from the writings of Bahá'u'lláh, instructions of the "Oneness of God, religion and humanity, teaching that all things are through prayer, fasting and meditation. This faith see themselves as world citizens, that encourages marriage, against drinking of alcohol, strong beliefs of meeting different people from all cultural and religious beliefs to work towards world peace, love and religious harmony through prayer, fasting and meditating. Through the importance of prayer, fasting and meditation is within the teachings that that Deliverance of souls, from the bondage of self, while purifying one from any attachments and distractions of the higher Gods and that privacy hath been enjoined while in fasting, meditation of quiet devotional moments to give oneself their full attention to the remembrance of God to connect with the spirit of God to bring in positive radiance into a positive direction of a great fulfilling life through the importance of fasting, prayer and meditation to manifest healthy wellness and creating healthy lifestyles for all humankind.

Write your truths before you start your meditation. Read meditation scriptures. Write your daily prayer out after your meditation of 3-6 hours. Allow time to write daily prayer. Be careful of food intake after meditation and fasting. Make sure you are mindful of negative people and communications deposited into your mind, body and soul while meditating and fasting for 30 days. Remember before you can manifest good, I have come to learn that I had to fast, purge and cleanse out all negative unwanted harmful energy. This is the approach I took and master while in writing of this journal that led into me creating my holistic organic products for this journal.

TRUTHS: DATE:

TRUTHS: DATE:

TRUTHS: DATE:

_____
_____
_____
_____
_____
_____
_____
_____
_____
_____
_____
_____
_____
_____
_____
_____
_____
_____
_____
_____
_____
_____
_____
_____
_____
_____
_____
_____
_____
_____
_____
_____
_____
_____

TRUTHS: DATE:

TRUTHS: DATE:

_____

_____

_____

_____

_____

_____

_____

_____

_____

_____

_____

_____

_____

_____

_____

_____

_____

_____

_____

_____

_____

_____

_____

_____

_____

_____

_____

_____

_____

_____

_____

_____

TRUTHS: DATE:

TRUTHS: DATE:

_____

_____

_____

_____

_____

_____

_____

_____

_____

_____

_____

_____

_____

_____

_____

_____

_____

_____

_____

_____

_____

_____

_____

_____

_____

_____

_____

_____

_____

_____

_____

_____

_____

_____

_____

TRUTHS: DATE:

_____
_____
_____
_____
_____
_____
_____
_____
_____
_____
_____
_____
_____
_____
_____
_____
_____
_____
_____
_____
_____
_____
_____
_____
_____
_____
_____
_____
_____
_____
_____

TRUTHS: DATE:

TRUTHS: DATE:

_____
_____
_____
_____
_____
_____
_____
_____
_____
_____
_____
_____
_____
_____
_____
_____
_____
_____
_____
_____
_____
_____
_____
_____
_____
_____
_____
_____
_____
_____
_____
_____

FORGIVENESS: DAYS 11-20

Now that you have faced your truths. Faced your wrongs and moving into the direction of full repentance, you are ready to move into forgiveness of yourself and asking forgiveness of others you have wronged, to be free, to establish peace, gain favor from God and walk upright in faith, leaving the past behind, the old life, negative people energy behind; releasing yourself to move into self-balancing, great harmony with the higher God, trusting and believing on faith as you dust off from old people, places and things, never to be found in toxic negative energy.

Anyone can backslide, strong Christian do struggle, but a true individual Christian will not remain in a state of mind of backsliding, and through meditation and fasting God will carry his children to full repentance and even discipline his children when on your life journey. When meditating and fasting in forgiveness know that God is always faithful and it is good to confess your sins daily for continuous release.

If you are unforgiving, it can turn you into being vengeful and bitter that can greatly affect and effect you and your life, your health, your mind, body and soul that pushes positive people close around you away from you, but most importantly it separates you from the great blessings of the higher God, and you must forgive others no matter what the offense; as some offenses may be very hard and difficult, but through fasting and meditation, you can and will learn to release to let go, let it go, let it go.

I repeat do not let others stagnate you to remain unforgiving, don't let others take your soul to hell on earth and hell on hell by being unforgiving. Let it go, let it go, let it go. So let's go!

FYI-Hell can be living on earth in anger, bitterness and unhappiness while living in the past as others are moving and growing stronger making great things happen positively for the person you are holding unforgiving ill feelings for. Let it go and forgive, healing in separation from people that hurt you is creating healthy boundaries, while healing in silence to make powerful moves. It is time to work on becoming forgivingly fit. If you have accomplished facing your truth, it is time to get into moving forward.

Meditation Scriptures to start with your truths:
1 John 1:9 "But if we confess our sins to him, he is faithful and just to forgive us our sins and to cleanse us from all wickedness."

Ephesians 4:32 "Be kind and compassionate to one another, forgiving each other, just as in Christ God forgave you."

Luke 6:37 "Do not judge, and you will not be judged. Do not condemn, and you will not be condemned. Forgive, and you will be forgiven."

Matthew 18:21-22 "Then Peter came to Jesus and asked, 'Lord, how many times shall I forgive my brother or sister who sins against me? Up to seven times?' Jesus answered, 'I tell you, not seven times, but seventy-seven times.' "

Mark 11:25 "And when you stand praying, if you hold anything against anyone, forgive them, so that your Father in heaven may forgive you your sins."

1 John 1:9 "If we confess our sins, he is faithful and just to forgive us our sins and to cleanse us from all unrighteousness."

Buddhism is powerful religion. A religion created by the founder Buddha Shakyamlini, who stated the "Awaken from the sleep of ignorance." Embracing life of all life without discrimination.

Meditation is powerful for the Buddhism religion focusing on the mental state of calmness, concentration, to be aware to hear positive vibrations into the mind and soul. When meditating is vital to understand that Buddhism study from the teaching of *Tripitaka*. The teachings is for one to be kind and nice to humankind, as one in this religion should seek to meditate to find inner peace that teaches once the mind is at peace, one can be free from mental and worry discomfort to attract the best of true happiness, to become a magnet to attract the best of living life conditions. One must learn according to Dharma, which means protection, it is vital that all in this religion must protect themselves from suffering that can come from daily living of life that originate in and through ignorance of no peace and Dharma method teaches one that eliminating ignorance is a practice. Buddhism famous quotes to meditate on:

1. "A disciplined mind brings happiness."
2. "Give, even if you only have a little."
3. "Conquer anger with non-anger. Conquer badness with goodness. Conquer meanness with generosity. Conquer dishonesty with truth."
4. "Delight in heedfulness! Guard well your thoughts!"
5. "If a man going down into a river, swollen and swiftly flowing, is carried away by the current — how can he help others across?"
6. "To support mother and father, to cherish wife and children, and to be engaged in peaceful occupation — this is the greatest blessing."
7. "Our life is shaped by our mind; we become what we think. Suffering follows an evil thought as the wheels of a cart follow the oxen that draw it. Our life is shaped by our mind; we become what we think. Joy follow a pure thought like a shadow that never leaves."
8. "If you meditate earnestly, pure in mind and kind in deeds, leading a disciplined life in harmony with the dharma, you will grow in glory. If you meditate earnestly, through spiritual

disciplines you can make an island for yourself that no flood can overwhelm."

9. "Good people keep on walking whatever happens. They do not speak vain words and are the same in good fortune and bad. If one desires neither children nor wealth nor power nor success by unfair means, know such a one to be good, wise, and virtuous."

10. "It is easy to see the faults of others, but difficult to see one's own faults. One shows the faults of others like chaff winnowed in the wind, but one conceals one's own faults as a cunning gambler conceals his dice."

Islam: This is also a very powerful religion, as this religion worship Allah, and teaches from the Quran. The most valuable thing I learned in this religion is the "Salat," which is a practice of daily prayers that this religion practice five times a day starting at dawn, noon, mid-afternoon, sunset and night. This teaching is practice meditation that the teachings states is greatly helpful to reduce stress, boosting the memory, while enhancing concentration and improving a strong and personal relationship with the higher God. Islam has a great way to encourage and embrace meditation with the following:

Reflection (Taffakur)-To think constructively with intentional purpose and positive outcome of greatness, remaining in the center of positive thoughts and not allowing your mind to drift off into negative thoughts.

Gratitude-Writing is an expression of gratefulness, which is how you will master this journal into a positive and better outcome of a great life. The Islamic faith believe is there is gratitude in your heart it leaves no room rom ingratitude. Always be thankful.

Seclusion-This is greatly practice in Islam, and the main thing you will need to master this journal to be effective in your life. The Islamic faith practice that seclusion will help one to remain focus and to tap into the sense of what is around one person life by breaking away from everything is liberating and a fulfilling balm to the soul while showing the importance of meditating alone, while being alone in silence to meditate to manifest great things into one's life.

The virtue of mindfulness in meditation that is practice that I have found to be very effective that leads to being conscious and aware in a good mental state without scattered thoughts is only through meditation in seclusion and silence. According to Al-Ghazali "If his intentions are true, his concerns are in order, and his diligence is improved, then he will not gravitate to his base desires and will not be preoccupied with idle thoughts related to the world. The reality of the truth will shine in his heart. (45).

If you make meditation, which is a simple regular habit, one will usher in positive results that will greatly accumulate over time into a pleasurable life.

Let's face it. Forgiving is hard. It is difficult and it can cause a lot of pain. Often humans chose to move it out the way quickly, or hold on to it that often causes one to make angry bad decisions, severe health problems that lead into becoming isolated to harbor unforgiveness longer, to become bitter, mean, cruel that bleeds on good people who has nothing to do with who caused the pain.

Learn to become "Forgivingly Fit"

Yes! You are now on your way. You have faced your truths, prayed about your truths, now you moving into forgiving others or yourself as you are now entering into becoming "Forgivingly Fit."

Forgiveness is not about the person that has wronged you. It is for you to step in a stronger psychological frame of mind to let it go; becoming positive for your inner self; not looking or seeking to do revenge to do or cause harm; and refraining from talking about the hurt, pain and individual that caused you to experience the unforgiveness.

Now you working on becoming "Forgivingly Fit." Be careful of your pride when working on becoming "Forgivingly Fit," it can cause resentment that can add to you remaining in an unforgiving state of mind set.

To remain strong and "Forgivingly Fit." Examine the individual that hurt you and sent you into unforgiveness state of mind; you will clearly be able to see the hurt, harm and long term wounds of the individual that caused you to be unforgiving; as the wounds of the individual could be a very difficult childhood from physical or sexual abuse, lack of parenting (no mother or father within the home), this is detachment which can destroy trust that sets a long term trajectory (path/trail) of isolation and loneliness and this causes conflict throughout one's life.

Last, to remain strong and "Forgivingly Fit," meditate and study the above scriptures on the forgiveness sections, surround yourself with strong wise supportive people who (Pastors, Evangelist) who have patience and non-judgmental that can help you understand the importance of remain strong in "Forgivingly Fit, "and the importance of seeking God's word to heal that only a higher God can and will do.

Write your forgiveness before you start your meditation. Read meditation scriptures. Write your daily prayer out after your meditation of 3-6 hours. Allow time to write daily prayer. Be careful of food intake after meditation and fasting. Make sure you are mindful of negative people and communications deposited into your mind, body and soul while meditating and fasting for 30 days.

FORGIVENESS: DATE:

FORGIVENESS: DATE:

_____
_____
_____
_____
_____
_____
_____
_____
_____
_____
_____
_____
_____
_____
_____
_____
_____
_____
_____
_____
_____
_____
_____
_____
_____
_____
_____
_____
_____

FORGIVENESS: DATE:

_____
_____
_____
_____
_____
_____
_____
_____
_____
_____
_____
_____
_____
_____
_____
_____
_____
_____
_____
_____
_____
_____
_____
_____
_____
_____
_____
_____
_____
_____

FORGIVENESS: DATE:

_____
_____
_____
_____
_____
_____
_____
_____
_____
_____
_____
_____
_____
_____
_____
_____
_____
_____
_____
_____
_____
_____
_____
_____
_____
_____
_____
_____
_____
_____

FORGIVENESS: DATE:

_____
_____
_____
_____
_____
_____
_____
_____
_____
_____
_____
_____
_____
_____
_____
_____
_____
_____
_____
_____
_____
_____
_____
_____
_____
_____
_____
_____
_____
_____
_____
_____

FORGIVENESS: DATE:

FORGIVENESS: DATE:

_____

_____

_____

_____

_____

_____

_____

_____

_____

_____

_____

_____

_____

_____

_____

_____

_____

_____

_____

_____

_____

_____

_____

_____

_____

_____

_____

_____

_____

_____

FORGIVENESS: DATE:

_____
_____
_____
_____
_____
_____
_____
_____
_____
_____
_____
_____
_____
_____
_____
_____
_____
_____
_____
_____
_____
_____
_____
_____
_____
_____
_____
_____
_____

FORGIVENESS: DATE:

_____
_____
_____
_____
_____
_____
_____
_____
_____
_____
_____
_____
_____
_____
_____
_____
_____
_____
_____
_____
_____
_____
_____
_____
_____
_____
_____
_____
_____
_____
_____
_____
_____
_____

FORGIVENESS: DATE:

_____
_____
_____
_____
_____
_____
_____
_____
_____
_____
_____
_____
_____
_____
_____
_____
_____
_____
_____
_____
_____
_____
_____
_____
_____
_____
_____
_____
_____
_____
_____

REPAIR, RENEW, RE-STAND: DAYS 21-30

Weeks 3-4 and you have faced your truths, you are cleansing and now into forgiveness, and this is your 3rd day and this last day should tell you if you need to move on into a constant meditation and fasting life cycle. Do I continue this daily? Should I invest in a planner? Should I invest in a journal? Should I adjust my diet? Should I change people, places and things?

Yes. You should do all of these things to "Repair, Renew and Re-Stand. If you have truly followed this manifestation journal you are now ready to:

Repair- What was broken can be fixed and healed in the higher God's name. You must admit you are broken in an area and work on the repairing to full restoration, through healing, speaking and spreading kindness in area of your life. Fix your flaws. We all have a flaw that can be repaired, if it is your attitude or your tone the way you talk or speak to people, self help yourself. This is a computerized world, YouTube has so many great positive learning tools you can deposit into your life to aid in the repair to renew to restand.

Renew- Learn patience! Take it slow and easy with yourself and don't rush yourself to self-learning to repair to renew to restand. Without patience, you invite frustration to come in that will lead to giving up and not following through to a full repair to renew to restand. To renew, you should work on your personal growth and self-esteem, you have to speak worthiness within yourself, while knowing and understanding you are a strong and unique individual well deserving of great things and speak high of yourself without the "arrogance and overly pride" which can lead to destruction. Renewing means you understand that the "sky" is the limited to renew and motivate yourself in a renewal of life as you repair to renew to restand.

Re-Stand- You are now stronger and ready as you have faced your flaws to repair, the first thing you must repair is you. You are the most important. Repair the relationship with yourself. Renew your relationship with yourself and be ready to restand. Come out of the devastating same life cycle of doing nothing, going nowhere, save yourself. Eliminate doubt! Trust yourself! Believe in yourself! Stop waiting on others to push and move you, get up to restand stronger.

Meditation Scriptures for repair, renew, restand.

Acts 15:16 after these things I will return, and I will rebuild the tabernacle of David which has fallen, and I will rebuild its ruins, and I will restore it. (FYI) Use your name where David name is to make it personal to repair, rebuild, and restand to restore yourself.

Job 42:10 And the Lord restored the fortunes of Job, when he had prayed his friend, and the Lord gave job twice as much as he had before. (FYI) use your name where Job name is to make it personal.

Peter 5:10 And after you have suffered a little while, the God of all grace, who has called you to his eternal glory in Christ will himself restore, confirm, strengthen and establish you.

Mark 11:24 Therefore I tell you, whatever you ask in prayer, believe that you have received it and it will be yours.

Visualization, Affirmations and Vision Board Techniques

The key to this 30 day fasting and manifestation journal one must first purge out all negative and wrongful energy and doings, nothing can manifest great with negative energy abiding within. Jump start your life into a positive direction by cleansing and purging. After you complete your 30 day process, it does not have to stop. You can add additional days following the jump start of this journal and add a personal scheduled journal, calendar and introduction of your own personal vision board to manifest great positive things into reality.

Visualization- Clear your mind. Get in a quiet place to clear all resistance and fear away from you and visualize you are there or have what you desire and walk in this every day. This is where you will need your journal and vision board. Be thorough as you envision your desires, and when deep into visualization you can connect and feel emotions. You cannot do in all in your head, you have to write it down and you must clear your mind and go deep in thought daily until it comes into your life. You now should have a clear vision after fasting and ready to manifest.

Affirmations- Establish an optimistic strong attitude with strong beliefs to see clear visualization while surrounding yourself with positive vibrations, sounds, communication and energy of other people that is negative can throw one off balance, a bad spirit is a bad spirit and a bad spirit is contagious and can cause strife and distraction and derail one from staying on track to reach positive goals while meditating and fasting. You are ready to manifest greatness!

Vision Board- Build your dreams. Set it in front of you and start to see the vision to manifest. Build your board, collect magazines, or clippings and photos from the internet and place them on your personal board and start you manifestation as you continue to fast and pray until you are able to put your hands on it.

REPAIR, RENEW, RE-STAND: DATE:

REPAIR, RENEW, RE-STAND: DATE:

REPAIR, RENEW, RE-STAND: DATE:

REPAIR, RENEW, RE-STAND: DATE:

REPAIR, RENEW, RE-STAND: DATE:

REPAIR, RENEW, RE-STAND: DATE:

REPAIR, RENEW, RE-STAND: DATE:

_____

_____

_____

_____

_____

_____

_____

_____

_____

_____

_____

_____

_____

_____

_____

_____

_____

_____

_____

_____

_____

_____

_____

_____

_____

_____

_____

_____

_____

_____

_____

_____

_____

REPAIR, RENEW, RE-STAND: DATE:

REPAIR, RENEW, RE-STAND: DATE:

REPAIR, RENEW, RE-STAND: DATE:

MANIFESTING THROUGH GOAL SETTING

It is time you know "Don't watch me, watch God." Moving on, release of letting it all go, it is now time to watch God do great things in your life. It is time to manifest long term manifestation. It is time to set goals, while expressing gratitude of expectancy to come. It is time to "Navigate Effectively Eloquently Composed with Yahweh." What are your goals after completing this fasting manifestation journal?

> ➤ N-avigate
> ➤ E-effectively
> ➤ E-loquently
> ➤ C-omposed
> ➤ Y-ahweh

When you faced your truths and wrote you letter to God, it was then that you should have come to realize that "what you sow, you reap." Karma, some call it, it does come back, and with a vengeance, whatever, you put out in the universe is another way many say it, it all comes back. If you planted good, good comes, if you planted wrong, it comes back. It is time to give and give without expecting anything back or bragging or boasting about what you did or have done, I have seen and learned when bragging, boasting, it creates a bigger lost. The most powerful things I learned is when negative thoughts enter into your mind and you later execute the negative thoughts to happen, you have created a powerful action that one may not be able to undo.

If you think privately about stealing, breaking into a home, and you later execute it out, you have created an action to return back unto you, meaning this could be police charges or murder upon yourself. If you think privately about torturing or taking someone by attacking their character, job, things to make one have hard times, and you later execute it out, you have created an action to return back unto you, meaning, you attacked and wanted someone to lose their job, you suddenly lose your job, you attack someone through lies, betrayal of lies, you suddenly become the topic though harsher lies and betrayal that can be filled with long time shame, humiliation and pain.

It is vital that people understand that until they cleanse through fasting, it is impossible to manifest good or greatness. How do you expect that will happen? If you have not face truths of wrong doings, cleanse, purge, forgiveness and atonement of any wrong doings. Number one way people fail is this famous saying "he/she did it to me, I am going to do it to him or her." This is the easiest way to lose everything, precious things dear to you by seeking revenge. It is a killer of self!

The higher God is soft, kind, loving, forgiving, eloquent and composed. God is gentle. God is a giver! God is soft and sweet! Set a goal to build positive and encouraging reading that is full of spiritual connecting energy to glow and grow. Think SMART to build SMART.

Universal Manifestation Journal Goal Setting Strategies:

✓ Glow to grow, grow to glow
✓ Setting goals establish a strong visual to reaching goals
✓ Disconnect from all negative energy and people for healthier and positive goal settings
✓ Establish healthier eating habits. Establish set times. This is important. Stay consistent on the set times of consuming food. This is the time you will want to look at your diet
✓ Establish heathier exercise time, meditation, yoga. Build the mind to glow and grow in a positive mindset to achieve goals
✓ Be sure to set SMART goals:
  o **Specific** goals that are clear with the intent to achieve
  o **Measurable** goals that you can track to reach

- o **Attainable** goals that you can reach. If you need to include someone in your attainable goals (coach, mentor), reach out to connect and identify your attainable goals
- o **Realistic** goals that are achievable that will not cause you to give up, quit or become overwhelming to lead to failure
- o **Timely** goal reaching should have a deadline, a time frame of reaching your goal to remain SMART.

Let's start with fasting. Many people fast for many reasons such as:

1. Healthier eating styles. Many people began the journey into healthier eating by researching healthier foods, cooking shows learning to cook healthier foods.
2. Stop smoking cigarettes, illegal drugs, or heavy consumption of alcohol. Many people will join ministries, volunteer in positive environments for support to help reach life changing goals.
3. Deeper spiritual connections. Many people are soul searching, seeking a religious base ministry to become committed into deepening spiritual connections with a higher God. Many are seeking to become forgivingly fit and atonement while fasting, purging and cleansing spiritually.
4. Job promotion. Many people will connect with people in various departments they are reaching or desiring to get the job promotion.
5. Educational growth. Going back to school to receive a GED, trade, or high college degree.
6. Negative forces, unwanted strong negative energy. This could be a bad mindset that one may have within themselves, desiring to stop strong use of profanity, pornography, selling of illegal drugs, and embedded hidden molestation. Molestation could be something forced upon you or you

forced upon someone. All of the above are strong negative energy that can hold one back in life for reaching true divine revelation of manifestation of greatness. *Psalm 147:3, he heals the brokenhearted and binds up their wounds. (KJB).*

7. World leaders, political leaders or job leadership.
8. Health illness. Many have found relief in serious health illness to be unfound. To have a healthy long life.
9. Family and friend, husband, wife, children, grandchildren you individual self.

There are many things one can fast for. Fasting should not be for *crazy motives* such as being successful in selling drugs to become a king or queen pin, destructions on or to human lives, greed of money or materialistic things.

Fasting Goals. What days will you fast? What are you fasting for? How long will you fast?

Today's Date	Target Date	Start Date	Date Achieved
Goal:			

1.	SPECIFIC: What you want to achieve/accomplish?	
2.	MEASURABLE: Knowing when you reach this goal?	
3.	ACHIEVABLE: Keeping it real with effort and commitment. Do you a partner/resources? If so what and how will you make it happen to reach your goal	
4.	REALISTIC/RELEVANT: Why is this goal relevant/significant in or to your life?	
5.	Timely: Setting realistic timeline/frames. What are your times?	

Start Time_____ End Time_____

Manifestation/meditation goals. What days will you do this? What are you meditation and desiring to manifest? How long will you do this?

Today's Date	Target Date	Start Date	Date Achieved

Goal:	
1. SPECIFIC: What you want to achieve/accomplish?	
2. MEASURABLE: Knowing when you reach this goal?	
3. ACHIEVABLE: Keeping it real with effort and commitment. Do you a partner/resources? If so what and how will you make it happen to reach your goal	
4. REALISTIC/RELEVANT: Why is this goal relevant/significant in or to your life?	
5. Timely: Setting realistic timeline/frames. What are your times?	

Start Time_____   End Time_____

Personal goals. What are you now striving for that contributes to you as a better person? What do you want to achieve?

Today's Date	Target Date	Start Date	Date Achieved

Goal:	
1. SPECIFIC: What you want to achieve/accomplish?	
2. MEASURABLE: Knowing when you reach this goal?	
3. ACHIEVABLE: Keeping it real with effort and commitment. Do you a partner/resources? If so what and how will you make it happen to reach your goal	
4. REALISTIC/RELEVANT: Why is this goal relevant/significant in or to your life?	
5. Timely: Setting realistic timeline/frames. What are your times?	

Start Time_____ End Time_____

CONNECTING WITH GOD

Now that you have complete this 30 day fasting and journal you have one last thing to complete. Now that you spent the last 30 days writing out your truth, facing your wrong doings, you went into becoming forgivingly fit and wrote in your journal, and went into the repair and renewing of yourself, learned the relaxing products utilized during the weeks of this journal, it is time to finalize you 30 days of writing and mailing the letter.

This is one of my personal favorites. I always begin my letter out "Dear God." I write a letter to God. I number the things I write to God, I talk to God through a letter and write down everything to God, I write what I did wrong and ask for forgiveness, I come clean in my letter to God, then I write what I desire from God. I always leave room to high light when things manifest into reality so I can highlight and date all that manifest into reality.

God is a big God to me. After I write it all out to God, I seal it and put it in the book of Deuteronomy 28, focusing of the first 13 verses of the 28th chapter, and leave it there for 3 days. After the third day, I seal it up and mail it to God and address it to me.

While the letter is out traveling in the mail. I began a fast the day that I mail the letter. I start a fast for 3 day for 3 hours. While the letter is traveling to get back to me, I am praying, fasting, meditating. I do not open the letter until I have completed my 3 day fast.

The letter you write should be deep and personal and only for you to read. After you have fully completed this fasting and manifestation journal, you should see manifestation into reality of greatness. Finalization and completion of this fasting and manifestation journal is writing and mailing the letter.

*For a full list of resources and bonus material make sure you grab your paperback copy of the *Universal Manifestation Journal.* *

ABOUT THE AUTHOR

Ms. Monica Earl Washington, nick name *"Neecy,"* short for Monica's middle name Denise was born in Fort Campbell, Kentucky and raised outside of Fort Campbell, Kentucky in Clarksville, Tennessee, graduating for the legendary Burt Junior High School, where she later moved into her high school years of Northeast High School, Class of 1983. It is at Burt Junior High School, Monica found her passion for writing and learned to keep private dated and organized journals of her daily life as a growing and developing young woman living in a small rural non-diversity southern town; desiring to navigate and take on the world in a busy unknown world directly after high school; while seeking her passion to unite stronger with diversity that was introduced unto Monica through Fort Campbell, Kentucky.

Monica later navigated in the world after graduating high school in 1983 with a desire to travel independently to many wonderful cities and states, yearning to connect with more diversity of the world and to establish a deeper creation for writing while later learning to utilize the typewriter, with the ability to type 60 words per minute with only 2-3 errors in the middle 80's; which greatly enhanced her in the job fields for various leading working positions as well as leveling up her passion for writing; while learning to build her own personal portfolio and journal styles of writing. Monica's greatest travels landed her in Jacksonville, Florida, as Monica later moved into the Atlantic Beaches of Florida. A door of sunshine opened for Monica, as Monica reached what she craved "meeting people of diversity, Monica's oxygen and life line began."

Monica has earned an associate degree in Secretarial Science, which open greater doors for Monica to learn data and word processing, creating stronger job opportunities and sharpening her writing abilities. Monica also has many federal government certification training, and has completed 75 hours in Special Education from Florida College at Jacksonville. Monica was the previous owner of Queenrodney Christian Cleaning Services of Jacksonville, Florida, cleaning million dollar home for many elite clientele to include several NFL football players. Monica is currently the owner of "Neecy's Soft and Sweet Holistic Organic Southern Scents. Monica is the mother of two handsome sons' her oldest James "Tank" Earl and Reginald Kilo Banks, and the Gma of two beautiful angels Corinthian "Corey" Earl and Naomi Earl. Monica currently resides in Fort Washington, MD and works for the Washington Headquarters (Pentagon), loves to uber eat delivery when not working for the Pentagon to meet great people. Monica is a faithful member of the United House of Prayer for all people and is on the Junior Female Usher Auxiliary Board of Alexandria, VA, Monica's major Christian life line.

Monica famous saying, "Don't watch me, watch God!

www.ingramcontent.com/pod-product-compliance
Lightning Source LLC
Chambersburg PA
CBHW070449130626
46553CB00006B/2328